Natke

Who-who-who goes hoo-hoo-hoo?

Peter Schneider
illustrated by Gisela Schartmann
translated by Tim Chafer

First published 2012 by Speechmark Publishing Ltd.

Published 2018 by Routledge
2 Park Square, Milton Park, Abingdon, Oxon OX14 4RN
711 Third Avenue, New York, NY 10017, USA

Routledge is an imprint of the Taylor & Francis Group, an informa business

A catalogue record of this book is available from the British Library.

ISBN 9780863889226 (pbk)

Who-who-who goes hoo-hoo-hoo?

Peter Schneider
illustrated by Gisela Schartmann
translated by Tim Chafer

Routledge
Taylor & Francis Group

LONDON AND NEW YORK

One night the little hedgehog was awoken
by a strange sound:

"Hoo-hoo-hoo!"

He woke his mother and asked her,
"Who-who-who was that?"

"I don't know – now back into bed with you!"
"But Mommy, who goes 'hoo-hoo-hoo'?"
"Don't ask so many questions and sleep,
my child!" said the mother,
tucking in the little hedgehog.

Next morning the little hedgehog asked himself:
"What a strange sound that was last night!
I must find out who goes 'hoo-hoo-hoo'!"

The squirrel with the bare tail came along.
"Ca-ca-can you tell me who-who-who goes
'hoo-hoo-hoo'?" said the little hedgehog,
stuttering.

"Learn to talk properly first!" growled
the squirrel with the bare tail.
"And anyhow, anything that goes
'hoo-hoo-hoo' must be dangerous!"
And with these words the squirrel
scrambled up the tree.

"Now I really want to know who goes 'hoo-hoo-hoo'",
the little hedgehog thought and set off.
He met the hare with the missing ear.
"Ca-ca-can you tell me who-who-who goes 'hoo-hoo-hoo'?"
asked the hedgehog, stuttering again as he sometimes did.

"Take a deep breath and think before you
speak!" said the hare with the missing ear.
"And anyhow, anything that goes
'hoo-hoo-hoo' must be dangerous!"
And with these words the hare hopped away.

At the pond he met the snake with the
knotted tongue.
"Ca-ca-can you tell me who-who-who goes
'hoo-hoo-hoo'?" asked the hedgehog,
stuttering again as he sometimes did.

"Ts-ts-ts, you can't sssspeak properly. You musssst be afraid,"
the snake with the knotted tongue laughed.
"And anyhow, anything that goessss
'hoo-hoo-hoo' mussst be dangeroussss!"
And with these words the snake slithered away.

In the meadow he met
the wild boar with the bad leg.
"Ca-ca-can you tell me who-who-who goes
'hoo-hoo-hoo'?" asked the hedgehog,
stuttering again as he sometimes did.

"Make an effort to say it properly or else I'm not
going to listen!" said the boar with the bad leg.
"And anyhow, anything that goes 'hoo-hoo-hoo' must be dangerous!"
And with these words the boar limped away.

As the sun was going down the hedgehog met the little mouse.
"Ca-ca-can you tell me who-who-who goes 'hoo-hoo-hoo'?"
asked the hedgehog.
"Hey, you-you you just stuttered!" exclaimed the little mouse, surprised.
"Why, do you stutter too?" asked the hedgehog.
"I sure do. That's why no-no-nobody listens to me. And
some fo-fo-folks even make fun of me,"
the mouse replied.

"I'd just love to know who-who-who goes 'hoo-hoo-hoo',
but nobody will tell me," the hedgehog explained.
The mouse had an idea:
"Well, le-le-let's go into the forest and find out!"
And so they set off together into the forest.

By the time they reached the middle
of the forest, it was night.
The hedgehog whispered,
"Gi-gi-give me your hand, I'm afraid!"
"And I'm so sca-scared as well,"
chirped the mouse and trembled.

And suddenly they heard a deep, friendly voice:
"Hoo-hoo-hoo! Don't be afraid!"

"Who-who-who are you?" asked the little hedgehog.
"Why, I'm the owl and I stu-stu-stutter just like you!"

The hedgehog and the mouse spotted the owl
in the tree and saw his friendly face.

"I've got to ta-talk to you," said the owl.
"A terrible mmmmonster is on his way to the forest and wants
to eat up a-a-all the animals. You've got to warn them!"
"Even the animals that make fu-fun of us?!"
asked the hedgehog.
"Yes, you've got to sa-save them all!" the owl hooted.

"No-no-nobody will take us seriously because we stutter,"
the mouse objected.
"This is what you've got to do," said the owl and whispered
his plan to the hedgehog and the mouse.
"Yes, that's just wwwwhat we'll do tomorrow!"
exclaimed the hedgehog and the mouse, and while they
slept that night, the owl watched over them.

Next morning the hedgehog and the mouse went to the squirrel with the bare tail. "A huge mo…"
"Talk properly first!" the squirrel butted in and started to scramble away.
"Le-le-let me finish and listen to me. It's very important!"
"Everybody knows that stutterers are liars," the squirrel growled.
"You-you-you bare-tailed squirrel," the hedgehog cried angrily, "what do you know about stu-stuttering?
Stop and llllisten!"

So the squirrel stopped and listened.
"A huge monster is coming and wa-wants to eat all the animals. Come with us and help us!"
"Sorry," the squirrel answered timidly, "right now I've got to … go and hide my nuts!"
"Bu-but we only have a chance if you help us!" cried the hedge-hog and the mouse, so the squirrel went along with them.

Together they ran to the hare with the missing ear.
"A huge mo..."
"Take a deep breath and think before you speak!"
said the hare and started to hop away.
"Le-le-let me finish and listen to me. It's very important!"
"Everybody knows that stutterers are dumb!" the hare mumbled.
"You-you-you one-eared hare," the hedgehog cried
indignantly, "what do you know about stu-stuttering? Stop and
listen!"
So the hare stopped and listened.

"A huge monster is coming and wa-wants to eat all the animals.
Come with us and help us!"
"Sorry," the hare whispered fearfully, "right now I've got to ...
count my carrots!"
"Bu-but we only have a chance if you help us!" they cried, so the
hare went along with them.

Then they all ran to the snake with the knotted tongue.
"A huge mo ..."
"Ts-ts-ts, you sssstill can't ssssspeak properly,"
said the snake and started to slither away.
"Le-le-let me finish and listen to me. It's very important!"
"Everybody knowsss that ssssstutterers are cowardssss!"
the snake hissed.

"You-you-you old knotted-tongue snake," the mouse and hedge-
hog cried angrily, "what do you know about
stu-stuttering? Stop and listen!"
So the snake stopped and listened.
"A huge mo-monster is coming and wants to eat all the animals.
Come with us and help us!"
"Ssssorry," the snake flicked his tongue nervously, "right now I've
got to ... keep an eye on my frogssss!"
"Bu-but we only have a chance if you help us," the animals cried, so
the snake went along with them.

Finally, they came to the wild boar with the bad leg.

"A huge mo …"

"Take a deep breath and think before you speak!" the boar grunted and started to limp away.

"Le-let me finish and listen to me. It's very important!" said the hedgehog.

"Everybody knows that stutterers are scaredy cats!" the boar snorted.

All the animals shouted: "What do you know about stuttering? Stop and listen!"

So the wild boar stopped and listened.

"A huge mo-monster is coming and wants to eat all the animals. Come with us and help us!"

The big wild boar mumbled anxiously: "I don't dare to, because the monster is bound to make fun of my limp."

Then, suddenly …

... they heard a terrifying roar accompanied by slurping and snorting noises. And the mouse had just managed to explain the plan to the other animals when the huge monster appeared.

The animals knew what they had to do.
They climbed on top of each other and shouted and
screamed and hissed and stuttered at the tops of their voices. And
finally the owl swooped down and perched on top.
And this frightened the monster so much
that it ran away and was never seen again.

To celebrate, the happy animals had a big party and thanked the hedgehog, the mouse and the owl. They sang and danced with the three of them and nobody ever made fun of them again.

About Who-who-who

This is a book to encourage children who stutter, their nonstuttering friends and all the adults who are connected with them. Even though the causes of stuttering are not completely understood, one thing we know for sure: children who stutter know exactly what they intend to say but stuttering disturbs their speech. Sometimes they get stuck in sounds, they repeat syllables and sounds or they prolong sounds, and often find it difficult to avoid a negative response from the listener. This difficulty can be compared to a situation, where you try to write neatly by hand and somebody else is hitting your arm again and again.

You can help children who stutter by listening actively. That means that you should show interest in what a child is saying (i.e. not the manner of how he/she is telling it). Adopting this approach will enhance the self-esteem of the child who will feel "What I am saying is important – no matter if I am stuttering!"

Sometimes the stuttering events are frequent, tense and with a long duration, - listeners become impatient, angry, concerned or feel helpless.
Having this reaction is common and can be used as an indicator that the child needs help and support via professional treatment.

Many parents are concerned that their child may be bullied because of stuttering. Indeed all children – with or without a stutter - are at risk of being teased, but this may well increase where a child stutters. Often this arises because the impatient or teasing adults or children have come up with their own incorrect perceptions about stuttering resulting in incorrect prejudices.

Some notes to take into consideration include:

- Stuttering is not a psychological disorder or a sign of a lack of intelligence
- Advice like "say that again correctly, take a deep breath before you speak, slow down, make more effort!" may reduce stuttering for the short term, but for the long term it can aggravate it.
- Only five children out of every hundred will stutter, usually because they have a disposition for stuttering. In some children stress may trigger stuttering. Other children have a major disposition and a trigger of any kind is not the underlying cause.
- "Don´t worry, the child will outgrow the stuttering, just ignore it" is not good advice. Unfortunately only two out of five children with a stutter will recover without intervention and of course it is often impossible to ignore stuttering. However children who present a severe stutter can ultimately lose their stuttering.
- Early treatment increases the chance to recover by up to 80%, but it provides no guarantee. However treatment can minimize the difficulties for both parent and child in cases where stuttering persists.
- Stuttering tends to occur in phases where it may be more or less pronounced.
- Parents are advised to inform nursery school, kindergarten, and primary school about any stuttering difficulties that the child may be experiencing.
- It is important to be able to discuss with your child any negative reactions such as teasing or bullying that he/she may be experiencing resulting in unhappiness about speaking or negative reactions from others. Discussing a planned approach to tackle this with teachers is very important showing support for your child and helping with self-esteem.
- Above all this book addresses stuttering children who may already have had bad experiences as a result of their stuttering. This book provides what may prove a very welcome, opportunity for a child to talk openly about previously unaddressed experiences.